Holidays

Veterans Day

by Rebecca Pettiford

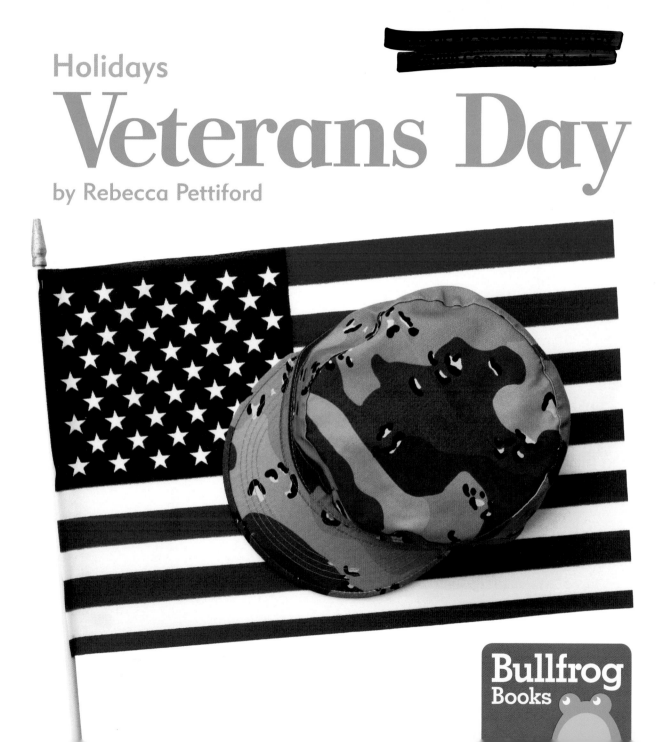

Bullfrog Books

Ideas for Parents and Teachers

Bullfrog Books let children practice reading informational text at the earliest reading levels. Repetition, familiar words, and photo labels support early readers.

Before Reading

• Discuss the cover photo. What does it tell them?

• Look at the picture glossary together. Read and discuss the words.

Read the Book

• "Walk" through the book and look at the photos. Let the child ask questions. Point out the photo labels.

• Read the book to the child, or have him or her read independently.

After Reading

• Prompt the child to think more. Ask: Do you have a veteran in your family? What sorts of things could you do to thank veterans for their service?

Bullfrog Books are published by Jump!
5357 Penn Avenue South
Minneapolis, MN 55419
www.jumplibrary.com

Library of Congress Cataloging-in-Publication Data

Pettiford, Rebecca.
 Veterans day / by Rebecca Pettiford.
  pages cm
 ISBN 978-1-62031-188-2 (hardcover: alk. paper) —
 ISBN 978-1-62496-275-2 (ebook)
 1. Veterans Day—Juvenile literature. I. Title.
 D671.P48 2016
 394.264—dc23

2014041414

Editor: Jenny Fretland VanVoorst
Series Designer: Ellen Huber
Book Designer: Michelle Sonnek
Photo Researcher: Michelle Sonnek

Photo Credits: All photos by Shutterstock except: a katz/Shutterstock, 10; Alamy, 16–17; Anthony Correia/Shutterstock, 11; iStock, 5, 8–9, 15, 18, 22tr, 23mr; SuperStock, 3, 18–19; Thinkstock, 6–7, 23ml, 23tl.

Printed in the United States of America at Corporate Graphics in North Mankato, Minnesota.

Table of Contents

What Is Veterans Day? 4

Symbols of Veterans Day 22

Picture Glossary 23

Index 24

To Learn More 24

What Is Veterans Day?

Veterans Day
is November 11.

What do we do on this day?

We thank people in the armed forces.

Why?

Our soldiers protect us.

They keep us safe.

We love our country.
How do we show it?
We hang a flag.

Look! It's a parade!

Veterans carry flags.
They wear their uniforms.

What is on the man's coat?

His medals.

How did he earn them?

He was brave.

Kay sees a man
in a rest home.

He fought in a war.

She says "Thank you."

15

Mark is at a cemetery.

It is for soldiers.

He plants a flag.

Mom is a soldier.

She was far away.

Hooray!

Mom is home!

Thank you for your service!

Symbols of Veterans Day

flag

soldier

medals

veterans cemetery

Picture Glossary

armed forces
People who serve in any of the branches of a country's military.

rest home
A place where old or weak people are cared for.

hang
To put an object up high so people can see it.

uniform
Special clothes that people who belong to a group wear.

parade
An outdoor march that celebrates a special day or event.

veterans
People who are or used to be in the armed forces.

23

Index

armed forces 6

brave 12

cemetery 17

country 9

flag 9, 11, 17

medals 12

parade 10

rest home 14

service 21

soldiers 6, 17, 18

uniforms 11

war 14

To Learn More

Learning more is as easy as 1, 2, 3.

1) Go to www.factsurfer.com

2) Enter "Veteransday" into the search box.

3) Click the "Surf" button to see a list of websites.

With factsurfer.com, finding more information is just a click away.

24